Colour
in the
Darkness

Helpful hints for people who
are feeling down

By Pam Norman

www.colourinthedarkness.co.uk

First Edition Published in 2006 in the UK
by Comfort Books
PO Box 3937
Bath
BA1 0BR
www.comfortbooks.co.uk

ISBN 0-9551874-0-0
ISBN 978-0-9551874-0-7

British Library Cataloguing Publication Data
A catalogue record for this book is available
from the British Library.

Book design by Sarah Heppenstall

Printed by The Bath Press, Bath

Dedication

This book is dedicated to
my brother Stephen Rawson and to my dear
friend Jenny Garrett who helped me through
my time of darkness.

Acknowledgments

With grateful thanks to my husband Michael,
daughters Jenni and Pippa and to Deborah
Wearing for their support and encouragement,
and to David Chambers, Lee Owen, Jackie
Short and Michelle Fillingham for their
practical help.

CONTENTS

FACE YOUR FEELINGS

Each day give your
feelings a number

**1... is despair
to
10... is normal**

Write these in your
diary to keep track of
your progress

Decide what you can
and cannot do at
the moment

"Be realistic"

Work out the
situations which
make you feel
stressed

Avoid them if possible

Determine not to feel bad about the things you can't do

"You have enough to deal with without adding guilt"

4

Make the most of
your best time of day

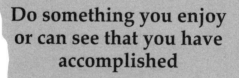

**Do something you enjoy
or can see that you have
accomplished**

If the world is beginning
to crowd in on you

"concentrate on one
thing at a time"

Don't agonise about why you feel the way you do

There may be no obvious reason – these things happen

If you find planning ahead difficult

don't do it

You may feel
overwhelmed at
times

"The feeling will pass"

Keep busy if you
have the energy

This will distract you
from those
inward-gazing thoughts

10

Laugh at yourself
occasionally

if you can

Don't listen to negative thoughts

Tell them where to go – out loud

Avoid situations
that make you
feel wobbly

**Take the least busy
routes and keep away
from deep water
and heights**

Don't hold all your
emotions inside

"Be honest about how
you are feeling"

Keep reminding
yourself that things
will get better

"Refuse to lose hope"

Look for something good about your situation

Be determined to find something, no matter how small

When you feel angry
or tense

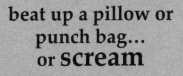

beat up a pillow or
punch bag...
or **scream**

Acknowledge your feelings

"You will be freer to understand them if you do"

If you feel unwell
or unable to
cope at work

**seriously consider
taking time off sick**

Illegal drugs are not
a solution

"they may make things
worse"

Go easy on yourself

"Don't try too hard"

If you have
suicidal thoughts

this is a symptom of
severe depression.
Tell your Doctor

If possible, put off
major life changes

**until you are
feeling better**

Write down how you feel on the good days

Then you can remind yourself of this on the bad days

For every negative
there is usually
a positive

Focus on the latter

When you are
feeling desperate

make it a rule to tell
somebody – don't keep
it to yourself

If your thoughts
keep going round in
circles, say them
out loud

**Verbalising things can
make them clearer**

Mope from time to time

Feel sorry for yourself – it is allowed

When you feel
drawn into danger

**acknowledge how you
feel, then walk away**

Don't dance with danger

**It is a risky thing to do
and you may regret it**

Make your body obey your mind in the morning

"Get out of bed and eat breakfast"

Give yourself a break

Get away from the things that pressure you for a time

If you know what
has caused you to
feel down

**ask yourself if you can
do something about it**

Get angry
with the depression

Tell it that it won't
win – anger is a more
powerful emotion

Cut down on the
amount you
are doing

"The less you have to
cope with, the better"

When you feel
you are making
progress, don't get
too busy again

"One step at a time"

Alcohol can have a
depressive effect

"Don't drink too much"

Remember that you
only need enough
strength for today

**"Tomorrow is
another day"**

If you have thoughts
about ending it all

it may be because part
of you wants to escape

If you hear voices

tell your Doctor

If you are feeling
worse as days go by

**do something about it
– get help**

Survive

Sometimes that is all you can do

Around one in
four people will
suffer some form of
mental illness during
their lifetime*

You are not alone

You may no longer
look forward to
the future or find
enjoyment in
anything

**These are symptoms of
depression**

The worst thing
about depression

is not having any control
over the way you feel

Many of the world's most inspired people suffered with depression

You are in good company

There are degrees of
depression – mild,
moderate and severe

**Which, if any, best
describes yours?**

Little things may
completely throw
you at the moment

**Anxiety and inability
to cope are signs of
depression**

Time can seem to
pass incredibly
slowly

for people who are
feeling down

Recovery may not be immediate

It can be like a roller coaster – lots of ups and downs before you get there

Mornings can be
cruel when you
wake up and you are
still feeling down

"Hang in there"

If you have a
stressful job or
young children

you may be more
vulnerable to depression

Remember, it is okay
to feel depressed

**It's not nice,
but it's okay**

53

If you have a
cold or the flu

You are likely to feel
lower because your
body is trying to fight it

Chronic illness
can cause depression

"The two go
hand in hand"

If you have felt
down for weeks
it may be due to a
chemical imbalance
in your brain

**Medication can restore
that balance**

56

If you are thinking about *how* you would end it all

"That is a danger sign – get help"

Bereavement is
a major cause of
depression

No wonder you feel
dreadful – you have lost
someone you love

It is hard to admit
that you are
depressed

"but doing so will
enable you to move
forward"

Depression is a
physical disease too

so your whole body may
not feel right

60

If you are worse
in the winter you
may have Seasonal
Affective Disorder

"Look into it"

You may feel
better from around
nine o'clock in
the evening

**Make the most
of this time**

Depression is an illness rarely spoken about

"Change that"

Post-natal
depression can
develop immediately
after having a baby

or it may begin
months later

Frustration can cause depression

Are you being held back in some way?

Because of the nature
of depression

your character traits
and natural tendencies
may be exaggerated at
this time

You can start imagining all sorts of things when you are depressed

"Voice your concerns to someone"

Depression can make you forget what it's like to be well

Be reassured – you will feel normal again

Men and women
get depressed

though the former are
less likely to seek help

If you have reduced
your medication and
feel low again

When you increase it,
it may take a while
before you feel
the effect

Depression can be
like a friend

if you have suffered
from it for a long time

A change of appetite
is normal when you
are depressed

If you are losing weight,
try watching television
or reading to distract
yourself as you eat

Sexual appetite is
often reduced

**Tell your partner so they
can begin to understand**

Depression is an
invisible illness

Don't despair, there is
a cure and people
do get better

YOU AND OTHERS

Get all the help you can

"Do not go it alone"

Confide in a
trusted friend

or someone who
has had depression

See your
Doctor regularly

"They are there to help"

Children are a great distraction

Although they make life tiring, they keep the days rolling along

When people irritate
and annoy you

**look for the good
in them**

Read advice leaflets
and books about
your condition

if you find that helpful

If you are a
senior citizen

the charity Help the
Aged may be able to
offer you support

If you can't face
something which
you have to face

**Get someone alongside
to face it with you**

If you are finding it difficult to look at things logically

ask someone else for their perspective on things

If you have
continuing financial
problems, get some
debt counselling

**The problem won't just
go away on its own**

Talk to a friend about
how you are feeling

**"You need to tell
someone else all
about it"**

If you have young children, have a break from them weekly – even just for a few hours

Make it a priority, whatever the cost

Counselling
or Cognitive
Behavioural Therapy
may be beneficial

**"Keep your
appointments"**

If you are worried about any aspect of your health

it is best to get it checked out

Say no to new
responsibility

**unless the challenge is
what you need and you
feel well enough**

Think of something
you can do to help
someone else

**It is good to focus on
other people for
a change**

Accept help from
your friends

**This is the time you
need them most
- don't alienate them**

Consider getting a
little job or
doing some
voluntary work

**It may bring you out of
yourself and make you
feel better**

Explain to your
family or friends
how you feel

"Enlist their support"

You will be surprised
how many people
understand

Be straight with them
and ask about their
experiences

If you really
lack confidence in
your diagnosis

seek a second opinion

If you can't find
someone you know
who understands

join a group of people
who do

Avoid negative people

they can make you feel worse

When you are
feeling better

talk to your Doctor
about reducing your
medication

Tell others when you
need some space

**Your children, if you
have any, need to know
that too**

If someone tells you to pull yourself together, they have little understanding

"Find someone else to talk to"

100

Talk to someone on a
telephone help line

**If you can't get an
answer, keep trying**

If you are lonely,
make the effort to
meet new people

"You may find someone
special to keep you
company"

Get help dealing
with any problems in
your life

before they get worse

Holding grudges can make you ill

Even if you have good cause not to, forgive, forget and move on

Don't be too proud
to ask for help

**Pride gains you nothing
in the long run**

When people say "How are you?" and you don't feel like answering

Smile and ask them how *they* are

Don't let people
discriminate
against you

**Depression is an illness,
not a weakness
or an excuse**

The Citizens
Advice Bureau is
a good source of
information

Find out if they can give
you the advice you need,
or point you in the right
direction

If others don't seem
to understand, don't
blame them

you may have been like
them once

You need support at
this time

Don't suffer alone

Your friends will be
worrying about you
if they know you are
depressed

**Let them do what they
can to help**

Have a good cry

Sometimes it is difficult to cry but if you can it will help

It is normal to feel
unsociable

**so don't worry if you
don't feel like going out
as much as you did**

If you can't face a pre-arranged meeting - don't go

Ask someone else to give your apologies

Ask a friend to contact you daily when you are feeling very low

It is important that someone is aware of how you are

If you can't do the things you used to do, don't do them

Tell people you are not quite yourself at the moment

116

WHAT TO DO

Watch funny films or go to a comedy show

Laughing will be a good change for you

Eat healthily, exercise
gently, and rest

"Look after yourself"

Sit in a park and
listen to birdsong

"It will do you good to
be close to nature"

Give yourself an aim
every day

**even if it is as simple
as going out to buy a
newspaper**

Review your
achievements and
congratulate yourself

"Don't put
yourself down"

Look through old
photographs or
film footage

**Spend time
remembering**

Listen to different stations on the radio

It can be good company

Write down the
things that are
worrying you

They won't seem so bad
down on paper

Take advantage of
any sunshine

**or have some time
on a sun bed**

Curl up in an armchair

Put your feet up and relax

Give away things
you know you will
never use

**Let someone else benefit
from them**

Get out of the house

Sometimes it can feel like a prison

Spend time thinking
of the things you
would like to do
or places to visit

"Dream"

Learn some new skills

Look for local classes or consider doing a course at college or university

Draw a picture
of your present
situation and how
you want things to be

Share it with someone

Find a symbol that is
meaningful to you

**Keep it with you
through the
day and night**

Tidy your
cupboards, desk
or drawers

**It will feel good when
you finish**

Email or write
to a friend

Tell them about how
things really are

134

Decorate or rearrange

You will at least see a difference somewhere in life

Complete a
questionnaire about
depression on the
Internet

**Gain an objective view
about whether you have
depression or not**

136

If foreign languages
or playing an
instrument interests
you

**consider having lessons
or teaching yourself**

Participate in one-to-one sports

Team games can seem more daunting at the moment

Write a list of the
things you need to
do and start, one by
one, or a bit at a time

"Clear your head"

139

Go for a walk

"The fresh air will do you good"

Find an inspiring picture postcard

Put it up where you can see it during the day

Get involved in a
worthy cause

**though don't take on
too much**

Visit an art gallery
or museum

**Look closely at any
exhibits that
interest you**

Get serious in the kitchen

Cook, bake, invent and impress!

Have at least two long-term goals

One is to get well.
Think of other goals
and work your way
towards them

Appreciate the
things around you

Make colour your focus
for a day

Find a food you like and eat it

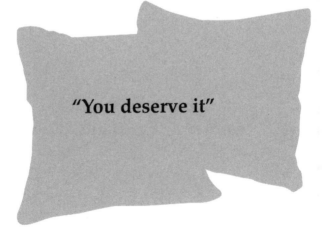

"You deserve it"

If you know what
will help you
get better

**do what you need to -
sooner rather than later**

The garden can be a sanctuary

Dig, plant, prune, weed – it is good therapy

Read in the bath

A bubble bath of course!

Make a list of the
things you can be
thankful for

Add to it each day

Be creative – write, construct, draw, paint, sew…

"Use your imagination"

If you are up early

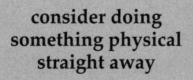

**consider doing
something physical
straight away**

Find things to take your mind off yourself and how you feel

"Distract yourself"

Treat yourself

**as a reward for
keeping going**

Borrow a good book
or audio book from
the library

It will help to take
your mind off things
for a while

Use your smile
muscles even if
you don't feel like
smiling

**It is good for the body
and the mind**

Hug a cushion,
a soft toy or a
willing person

**We all need comforting
physical contact**

Look out for local
events and plan to
go along

**Even if you don't make
it on the day, it is good to
have things in your diary**

Stroke your pet if
you have one

or borrow someone
else's for a day

If you feel up to it, consider having guests

It will be a distraction and give you focus

161

Find a new interest
or hobby

Buy or borrow a book or
magazine about it

If the day or week
stretches empty
ahead of you

plan things to fill it

Write yourself
reminder notes

**so that you won't forget
what you need to
remember**

You have got this far
– well done!

**Congratulate yourself
for keeping going
despite everything**

GOING DEEPER

Take in the beauty of
a flower – examine it
close up

**You are even more
marvellous than that**

Remember that you
are loved

**God loves you just as
you are**

Listen to some worship music

It may help to lift your spirits

Write a letter to God
about how you feel,
then read it to Him

It will crystallise your
thoughts and may
open up a whole new
life for you

God understands

He knows you better than you know yourself and He knows what you are thinking

Accept yourself as
you are

**God made you that way
and He has a plan for
you, if you let Him
take control**

You are not alone in
the middle of
the night

God never sleeps

Other people have
survived tough times
too

Read the Psalms to
see how they got
through them

173

Look for gems to
help you

**You will find some in
the book of Proverbs in
the Bible**

Consider the human body

You are unique, created by God

God can help, but
you need to ask

Ask someone to pray
with you or for you. Or
pray for yourself

Find a church which
is friendly and
welcoming

**Give yourself the
opportunity to
encounter God**

Refresh or strengthen your faith

Build up your beliefs by reading a modern version of the Bible

Resist the temptation
to do what you
know is wrong

God can help you
find another way if you
ask Him

Draw near to God
and He will draw
near to you

He has promised that
you will find Him if you
are earnestly looking
for Him

Discover more
about God

**Read about his son
Jesus' life and teachings
in the New Testament**

Make peace with
your Maker

**Put the past behind and
start to discover the
things He has
to offer you**

Don't give up – it's
as simple as that

"just don't"

HELPFUL WEBSITES

www.colourinthedarkness.co.uk
www.mind.org.uk
www.samaritans.org.uk
www.helptheaged.org.uk
www.netdoctor.co.uk
www.thecalmzone.net
www.alphacourse.org

TELEPHONE HELP LINES (UK)

SAMARITANS
08457 90 90 90

CALM (5pm – 3am)
0800 585858

CRUSE (for the recently bereaved)
0870 167 1677

Disclaimer: The publisher and author take no responsibility for actions taken as a result of reading this book or for the content of the websites listed. The organizations on this page do not necessarily reflect the views and beliefs expressed in this book.

* Source: Goldberg, D. & Huxley, P. 1992, Common mental disorders a bio-social model, Routledge. London and New York

Give the gift of **Colour in the Darkness**
to your family and friends.

Comfort Books
PO Box 3937
Bath
BA1 0BR

Write to the above address, enclosing your
name, address, number of copies required
and cheque or postal order payable to
Comfort Books.

Cost per book: £5.00 plus P&P
(Please add Postage & Packing of £1.00
per book for orders from within the UK)

Allow 28 days for delivery. Do not send
cash. Your details will not be passed on to
other organisations or interested parties.

To order online, for details of how to
order from abroad, for special offers and
multiple orders visit our website:

www.comfortbooks.co.uk